Menagerie Theatre Co...

presents

TWO INTO WAR

Gifts of War
by Fraser Grace

The Retreating World
by Naomi Wallace

War has never been so beautiful...

First performed at the Riverside Studios, London
on Tuesday 19 April 2005

National Touring Production opened at the Bristol Old Vic Studio,
on Monday 4 April 2005

Gifts of War
by Fraser Grace

Set in Athens as the beacons burn, signalling a
Greek victory over the Trojans.

NEMESIS: Jasmine Hyde
Directed by Paul Bourne

INTERMISSION

The Retreating World
by Naomi Wallace

Set during the UN embargo of Iraq,
between the two Gulf Wars of 1991 and 2003.

ALI: Kamaal Hussain
Directed by Patrick Morris

Above: Jasmine Hyde as Nemesis and Kamaal Hussain as Ali
(photograph by Diana Matar)

When we originally developed these plays they were totally separate pieces, part of a festival of work that had nothing to do with war, being two of a dozen monologues – apparently the only link was the solo voice.

Despite coming from such different writers, the plays became an obvious pairing in the frenetic countdown to the war in Iraq, opening (quite by coincidence) in the same week that the bombs began falling on Baghdad. Since then, they have become inseparable – growing in theme, in presence and in impact, each powerfully mirroring the other.

Both plays take us back in time: *The Retreating World* to the recent past of pre-war Iraq, after ten years of international sanctions; *Gifts of War* to the ancient, yet somehow more familiar, past of Athens at the end of the Trojan War.

Away from the clamour and glamour of journalistic reporting and comment, the plays reflect a war we may not recognise; No blood. No battles. No smoke. This is war carried on the tongue, waged in a glance, fought in silence.

Paul Bourne and Patrick Morris
Directors
Menagerie Theatre Company

Fraser Grace: Can War Keep its audience?

1 I am asked to join a panel discussing war plays.
2 I plead ignorance; I have never written a play about war.
3 Clearly I am in denial.

Alright I'll rephrase the statement: I have never *consciously* decided to write a play about war – why would I want to?

1 In war a character's choices have effortless significance – especially if he is a general, or say, a president.
2 (I overheard this one in a theatre one time) It's easy to be poignant about death.
3 War is a constant of the human condition, as constant as love or death – it has a limitless audience.

I make a resolution; I will nurse a conscious interest in war. I will examine its causes – psychological, emotional, political, ideological, 'spiritual', atavistic, banal, trivial – all the pressures which make a group of humans attempt the subjugation-by-force of another group. Not only will I get an audience, I'll be useful; humanity has an obvious interest in contemplating these causes because, after all...

Ah. In the words of Steve Turner:

History repeats itself.
Has to.
No-one listens.

Could this be where our theory crumbles....?

Fraser Grace 2005 /
History Lesson by Steve Turner
(produced with kind permission)

Iraq's ghost story

I was commissioned, along with five other writers, to write a 'ghost story'.

I had at that time, been thinking about an article I'd read by John Pilger, about how most Iraqis' had had to sell everything that mattered most to them, namely their heirlooms, in order to survive the economic blockade. And selling heirlooms to eat did not mean selling great and ancient treasures, but rather books that had been passed down from parents to children, a silver wedding spoon, a bracelet bought by a cousin on a trip to Europe decades earlier.

People were forced to sell their last pieces of personal history, the links that bound them from one dead loved one to the next, the simple objects that through decades had so patiently witnessed their lives.

Iraq lost more than 5% of its population due to the embargo, the equivalent of 14 million Americans. What equivalent to British lives? Five percent of its population. That's a lot of life gone. That's a lot of ghosts in Iraq, with 'made in the USA' stamped on their foreheads.

The present war and the ongoing occupation of Iraq is simply a continuation of the first Gulf War and the subsequent ten year embargo. This onslaught against an entire people for the last fifteen years has still to be reckoned with.

Naomi Wallace

Biographies

Fraser Grace

Fraser's first play *Perpetua,* produced by the Soho Theatre Company at the Birmingham Rep and published by Oberon Books, was the joint winner of the 1996 Verity Bargate Award. Other plays include *Cockayne*, commissioned by the Birmingham Rep and *Girl On a Tank* commissioned by SOHO. His next play *Breakfast with Mugabe* is being produced by the Royal Shakespeare Company.

Naomi Wallace

Naomi Wallace's work has been produced in both the United Kingdom and the United States. Her plays include *One Flea Spare*, *In the Heart of America*, *Slaughter City*, *The Inland Sea* and *The Trestle at Pope Lick Creek.* She is a recipient of the MacArthur Fellowship, and the Obie Award. Her new play, *Things of Dry Hours*, will be produced at NYTW in New York in 2006. Her award-winning film *Lawn Dogs* is available on DVD. She is presently working on a commission for the Royal National Theatre and the Guthrie Theatre of Minneapolis.

Jasmine Hyde

Jasmine trained at Pembroke College, Oxford and R.A.D.A. Her theatre credits include, *Pericles* (RSC/Cardboard Citizens), *Coast of Utopia* (National Theatre), *Charley's Aunt* (Northcott, Exeter), *Singer* (Tricycle Theatre), *Waters of the Moon* (Salisbury Playhouse), *Tiny Dynamite* (Frantic Assembly/Paines Plough at Traverse Theatre and On Tour). Jasmine has also appeared on Television in *Casualty* (BBC), in the films *Undo*, *Other* and *Restoration* and in over 100 radio plays for which she won the 2000/01 Carleton Hobbs Award

Kamaal Hussain

Kamaal trained at Central School of Speech and Drama. His recent theatre credits include, *Biscuits of Love* for Quiconque at Dublin and an Irish Tour, and *Macbeth,* as Macbeth at Forced Entertainment, Sheffield. Other theatre includes Ferdinand in *The Duchess of Malfi,* Aegeus in *Medea,* and Woodcutter in *Blood Wedding* at the Leicester Haymarket Theatre.

Paul Bourne, (Director; *Gifts of War*)

Paul is a freelance director and Artistic Director of Menagerie Theatre Company. He spent two years as the Artistic Director at Center Stage, New York and six years as a freelance director in Germany, Italy and Belgium. Credits include directing the European Premiere of David Mamet's *Oleanna* and the world premiere of Tennessee Williams' last short play *Williams' Guignol.* For Menagerie he has directed Steve Waters' *The Cull*, *The Gifts of War* by Fraser Grace, *Seeds* by Diane Samuels, *Sweetie Pie* by Anna Reynolds, *The Yellow Boat* by David Saar and *Hard Sell* by Craig Baxter.

Patrick Morris (Director; *The Retreating World*)

Patrick is Associate Director of Menagerie and currently directs their Writer Attachment Programme. He trained as an actor at Exeter University before moving to the USA for nine years where credits include *Henry VI* at New York's Public Theatre, Edward Albee's *Counting the Ways* directed by Joseph Chaikin, and *On the Razzle* working with Tom Stoppard. Work in the UK includes site-specific projects with Wrights and Sites, and national tours with Foursight Theatre, most recently playing Jason in their production of *Medea*. For Menagerie, he has appeared in *The Cull* by Steve Waters, *Hard Sell* by Craig Baxter and directed premieres of Naomi Wallace's *The Retreating World* and Claire Macdonald's *Correspondence*.

Andrew Lovett (Composer)

Andrew studied music at Cambridge University and composition at the Guildhall School of Music and Drama, London and City University, London. He currently teaches at Trinity College of Music in London. He specialises in electro acoustic composition, particularly combined with small groups of instruments or soloists. *Voyage* for ensemble and electro acoustic music, was performed by the London Sinfonietta of at the South Bank Centre, London in April 1999, conducted by Martyn Brabbins. *Unknown Terrors* for cello, keyboard and electronics was premiered by Judith Mitchell and Clive Williamson and broadcast on Radio 3 in April 2000.

Irene East (Casting Director)

Irene has cast theatre productions for The National Theatre, The Palace Theatre, Watford and The Tobacco Factory, Bristol. London productions include *Apache Tears* (joint winner Peggy Ramsay Award), *Pete 'N Me* (New End Theatre), *Picasso's Women* (Ambassador Group/Andy Jordan Prods), *Hard Times* (Love & Madness Prods), and *Hard Sell* for Menagerie. Films include *Tonight's The Night*, *A Long Way Home*, *The Contract*, *Second Hand* (First prize, Cannes Film Festival) and *Jealousy.*

Richard Matthews (Designer)

Studied fine art and illustration at Norwich School of Art. Has worked within the theatre and television industries for nine years as a designer, painter and props maker. Previously working for Norwich Theatre Royal, Glyndebourne Festival Opera and Openwide International.

Sherry Coenen (Lighting Designer)

Sherry studied at the University of Miami, Florida. She has designed productions in both the US and UK, most recently *Cargo* at the Oval House Theatre, London. She currently works as a technician at The Junction in Cambridge.

 menagerie

Menagerie is a leading independent producer of new writing for the stage. In addition to high quality commissioning and touring the company also promotes a wide range of theatre projects including the Hotbed festival.

www.menagerie.uk.com

Production Team
Producer: Alex Drury
Designer: Richard Matthews
Production Manager: Daisy O'Flynn
Costumes: Sue Pearson
Light Design: Sherry Coenen
Music/sound: Andrew Lovett
Casting: Irene East

ARTS COUNCIL ENGLAND
LOTTERY FUNDED

theatre503
LATCHMERE PUB

THE JUNCTION

TWO INTO WAR

GIFTS OF WAR by Fraser Grace
THE RETREATING WORLD by Naomi Wallace

BUTTERFLY FINGERS
by Fraser Grace

A STATE OF INNOCENCE
by Naomi Wallace

First published in this collection in 2005 by Oberon Books Ltd
521 Caledonian Road, London N7 9RH
Tel: 020 7607 3637 / Fax: 020 7607 3629
e-mail: oberon.books@btconnect.com
www.oberonbooks.com

Printed in Great Britain by Antony Rowe Ltd, Chippenham

Contents

TWO INTO WAR
Gifts of War
The Retreating World

GIFTS OF WAR

Character

NEMESIS

Menagerie's *Two Into War* production, which coupled *Gifts of War* with Naomi Wallace's short play *The Retreating World*, was first produced at The Latchmere Theatre (Theatre 503), in March 2003.

NEMESIS, Rachel Aspinwall

Directed by Paul Bourne
Designed by Idit Nathan

A bathroom. A doric column. A bath. A dressing table with a mirror, and a glass of wine. A window, with the blind down.

Off, disco music, voices, drinks, laughter.

As lights rise, a WOMAN is sitting at the dressing table, giggling to herself. She is elegantly dressed in a silk trouser suit with a mandarin collar, her face heavily made up, golden hair piled on her head.

Heroic Greece, Athens. What a city – country – race, I should say.

And I have been made so welcome here. Kindness like a shower of rain.

Can you hear them?

We're having a party, and Penelope – yes Penelope – Penny says, Cocktails, anyone?

I haven't had a cocktail for years, not for years and years, I'm lost, I am at a complete loss to know what to choose, what to ask for. Even the names are a mystery…the names are different in Athens anyway, and let's face it, names are half the fun with cocktails, as with the Greeks. Agamemnon, Aegisthus, Clytaemnestra – I can't imagine what they call their drinks – can you?

Penny says, what about this one; it's cider, it's something else, something else, dum de dah – Snakebite.

I don't know I say, I've never heard of it…

O go on she says it's not even a proper cocktail, this one. Try it.

So I do.

She giggles again.

I am in time for the celebrations, you see. They are all officer's wives – Penny, she's the wife of Odysseus, Odysseus who had the idea in the first place. The idea of the horse. And there's Barbara, Fiona, someone else, Chloe I think, and Clytaemnestra their Queen, she's here somewhere. Somewhere else, obviously, setting places at table according to Barbara, preparing a welcome for Agamemnon. A dinner, apparently, upstairs. A welcome fit for the victors, the incredible, clever Greeks. But the girls are having cocktails down here, having just spotted the beacon and heard news of victory, and I am invited because I am new. And because my husband, though not quite a Greek but an ally, has played his part, has helped end the hellish siege of Troy – not that anyone remembers my husband. Or his part. So I am invited, we – they – drink cocktails – and a game begins, it starts spontaneously because, as I say, I have no idea what to choose.

Try mine, try ours, try this one, go on, try it Darling…! So in the end, I drink, and keep on drinking – I take a sip from every glass. A big syrupy mouthful.

My head!

She giggles again – and again sobers.

The Horse figures large as you might imagine. Horse of Troy, Trojan Donkey, Horse Spit. They just keep mixing them up, making them up, for all I know. Horse Kick. Belly. Belly of the horse. Trojan widow, Trojan horse, Trojan tart. Fuck the Trojans. Whisky in that one, I think.

I drink all of them – I taste every last one. It feels so wonderful to be accepted, to be here, in Athens at last. To plant one kiss on every sticky glass.

She looks again in the mirror. She adds powder to her face.

Penelope – she is a classic Greek. Not beautiful exactly, but strong. And her husband, Odysseus-the-nimble-witted, well, he must be nimble witted, mustn't he? I mean, who…how could anyone have an idea like that? A giant horse full of… It's brilliant! After ten years of war. Ten years starving the Trojans into submission – a submission that never comes – and the answer Odysseus comes up with, is a horse.

As for the Trojans – how could they be so stupid?

My head is spinning. Ten, twelve cocktails? Twenty? I've no idea. And all these brilliant creatures, are swimming around me. Happy. Happy enough to embrace even me, a stranger. And me. Happy to be embraced, at last.

I need some fresh air after that.

Here, let me help you. It's Penelope. Her eyes are twin bonfires, torched by the brilliance of her husband, Odysseus. Odysseus-the nimble-witted. Nimble footed too, he's not home yet, though no doubt he'll turn up eventually, full of stories.

O they'll all still be in Troy says Barbara, Sacking the place, Celebrating. She's the leader of these women, that much is obvious. Let the boys have their fun, she says, they've earned it. And while the boy's are living it up in Troy, we'll have our fun, here – sisters, together…

Fresh air. Besides, I need to powder my nose again.

She dabs at her face with her makeup.

Drunkenness is one thing. As I say to Penny, we foreign girls have to think of appearances.

Better?

Yes. We'll do.

Lights down.

*

Lights up. The blind over the window is up. The Woman is now standing by the window, her glass in her hand.

Still no news of Fiona's husband, Patroclus. Still not home. He's not mentioned by any of the messengers, he could be dead or alive, Fiona has no idea.

Nor me, actually. I say, I've no idea about my husband, either. That's the way it goes with war.

Do you know, He writes to her every day. Penny again. Sitting here. Keeping me company.

Who does? Who writes every day?

Fiona's husband. Patroclus. And the letters stopped quite suddenly, so she knows something's wrong.

Perhaps Barbara's right, I think. Perhaps that's what's happening now, in Troy. Barbara's right, I say, I bet old Patroclus – whatever his name is – I bet he's with Odysseus, living it up. Trashing Troy. Enjoying soldiers' perks. No time to write a letter, what does she expect?

That's the upper ranks for you. Fields of paper, rivers of ink, oceans of noble sentiment.

I haven't had a single line from my husband since the day we parted.

Really?

Really. It's alright, I don't mind. I've learned to live without warnews. I've learned to prefer it.

She looks at me then, Penny. Ah, But it's different for you, she thinks. You're not a Greek. You don't feel as a Greek feels. We are closer to the gods, we have finer feeling – that's why they give us victory.

Can you believe it? The Trojans seriously opened the gates of Troy to a horse?

It was a giant horse, says Penny.

Yes, but still, a horse. Well. Let's hope he was well hung, I say.

She laughs at that. We both do, this Greek girl and I. We laugh and laugh. You can almost picture it: a silly giant horse, with a giant wooden prick. And its belly full of murder.

When I've had enough air, out here, we go back in, and straight away, we bump into Barbara. Or rather, Barbara bumps into us. Whoopsadeary.

You have a lovely house, here Barbara, I say.

Thankyou.

It's like the whole of the city of Athens, I say – it's so peaceful, so civilised.

I'm glad you like it. What's your house like? Do you have a house of your own in – where is it you come from? Naples isn't it?

Yes, Naples, I say.

Is it nice in Naples? In your house?

O yes, quite nice, I say, but not as nice as here.

Fruit. She says, yes, I remember now. You have lovely fruit, in Naples.

That's right. O Yes, I say. We love our fruit, in Naples, all kinds of fruit. In fact, Barbara, the more exotic the fruit, the better. I was just admiring that bowl of fruit in your bedroom. I hope you don't mind me taking some…

No no, she says. I'll show you the
she says, and I'll mix you another co
the girls are onto champagne now.

This place! When did I last drink champagne?
husband if he were here now, he would be astonish
And he'd love the games, I say, that's what first drew
him to serve with the Greeks, to serve you Athenians.
You're all such wonderful athletes.

I don't mention the intelligence, obviously.

It's hard to get over the intelligence, the cleverness of a
Greek. A horse you see, is the sign of Poseidon, god of
water, of the sea. The Greeks know their gods well
enough, worship them as they should, but the
Trojans…well, as Barbara says, the Trojans are fanatics
darling, you can almost hear the fools falling to their
knees. O look! It's an offering for Poseidon, those feeble
Greeks want a safe journey home. So they've built an
offering and parked it here – look, their ships are off
round the headland already. They've gone! We are
delivered! Open the gate, bring the horse in, let's not
annoy Poseidon now, or he'll send destruction on us.
Bring the horse in, fetch flowers, wine, we'll make
garlands, pour libations…

Flowers? Libations? After ten years of siege there are no
flowers. There are not the roots of flowers. Everything in
Troy that can be eaten has been eaten. (*Incredulous.*)
Wine…?

Let it stay with us, this horse, this magnificent god,
inside Troy's walls. No Trojan has seen magnificence for
years, and he is magnificent, this Poseidon, even without
libations. A thing none can question. A great, immutable
God – he could crush a Greek with one flick of his hoof.

rest of the house later,
cktail, but I'm afraid

My
ed.

parties reach. It has
rits are fine as far as
without the
one of the other ships
memnon's, and a
No Odysseus, no sign
of course, there's still
d. My darling.

Singing – there's been quite a bit of that.

What can you sing?

Me, O, I don't know, girls, I'm not much of a singer

Ladies…give her a break, don't cramp the new girl.

No it's alright, Penny, I don't mind. Alright. I'll sing you a song. A song from my lovely homeland. A song of love and love lost, from the beautiful city of Naples.

They clap at that all right. I open my mouth and I sing, and my mouth is a mouthful of birds.

She shows us how it was; nothing escapes her lips but a dry, lost, breath, struggling to find voice; a thousand voices, screaming.

Her husband's missing. Leave it. We'll play a game instead.

Such kindness. Such…consideration, from a people I barely know.

Why don't we play spin the knife?

Now this is a game I have played. With boys, obviously, but the boys as I said are otherwise engaged – so it's just girls. Well we *are* in Greece.

All the ladies sit in a circle. A knife is placed in the middle and everyone takes a turn. Of course the Greek version – like everything else in mighty Athens – is rather more sophisticated than at home. One person – the one they call the Jolly – is chosen to be kissed by everyone else. Each girl spins the knife in turn, and only when the knife points to this Jolly person, does the spinner take their kiss. And the game goes on until everyone has had a turn. It can go on all night apparently, this game, and frequently does.

So we select our Jolly. It's all very democratic.

I vote for Barbara, since she's the leader, but everyone else, strangely, votes for me. They explain that the Jolly is kissed, in the Greek version, not in the open, not even behind a curtain, but away from the others, in a separate room altogether.

Barbara is the first to spin me. She touches my body in a way that is both expected, and alarming. I don't flinch.

Barbara is lady-in-waiting to Clytaemnestra as well as a general's wife and since it is common knowledge that Clytaemnestra has been having an affair with Aegisthus while her husband Agamemnon is away at war, Barbara is concerned the banquet being prepared above our heads – the banquet for Agamemnon – may not be entirely…vegetarian. Butter knives may not be the only blades being sharpened. At least that's what she tells Penny. What Barbara says to me is, I wonder, Darling, is meat on the menu, tonight? squeezing my pudenda hard on the word meat. And she breathes her hot, sweet breath, in my ear.

They are fastidious about their breath, the Greeks, as about all their bodily odours. It makes one quite conscious of one's own fragrance, one's own smell.

Penelope when it is her turn to kiss, is a real Greek, by which I mean, an athlete. A kiss with Penelope is a marathon – the important thing, for the recipient, is not to reach the finish first, but to participate, with gusto. And then shake hands firmly with the winner.

Fiona… Fiona, pecks my cheek shyly, her eyes cast down. I can see the life draining from Fiona by the minute, the strain of facing life without her Patroclus. When she's delivered her peck, she squeezes my hand, weakly: I am a sister in suffering, is what it means, this squeeze of the hand, and she turns to leave. You're not getting away with that I think, and I grab her spindly wrist, kissing her full on the mouth, as though I could push the life right back in again. Or something.

That's what we call a kiss in Naples, I say, and she stares at me, afraid.

Giggles. Sobers.

And then Barbara spins me a second time.

O Yes, Barbara, I groan, yes yes, meat is on the menu.

And I put out the light.

I have to fix my face all over again, after that.

Lights fade.

*

Lights up. The blind is down again. A candle has been lit. The WOMAN sits on the side of the bath.

Once it is dark, a man the Greeks have bribed – some wretched slave or traitor – pulls away a loose board in the side of the horse. Greeks bearing terrible gifts tumble out. By now their ships have turned round you see, and landed again. Warriors with swords stream in through the flapping gate. And then a second darkness falls, this great, civilising power falling on its enemy.

The usual rules are observed, the latest messengers confirm. The city itself is destroyed, Men – husbands – are unmanned, humiliated, slain, the Women raped – sisters, mothers, daughters, – then enslaved. The complete Athenian victory.

Did I tell you I came from Naples?

She removes her hair – underneath, her scalp is a mess of sores, and what remains of her own hair. She will sit with the wig in her hands.

Long before Troy falls, I have abandoned her. Smuggled out, to sail across oceans, come here, drink cocktails with the Greeks. And still, until I see the bonfires, until Greek messengers let fly their scalding sparks, I don't know what I'm missing. In a siege, the rule is you starve the enemy. Those who haven't died of the plague. And since plague is Troy's only remaining asset, we decide one night on a parting gift. I win that vote, too, because I am still the most beautiful, despite the disease, the strongest. I will remain contagious.

Poseidon, angered by their asinine abuse of his image, by their defiling treachery, gives me fast winds. Brings me here, safe, to Athens. Who says the gods are on the side of the Greeks?

After I have spun the knife with Barbara for a good twenty minutes, Penny comes up to me with an odd look on her face. Odd because uncertainty was never meant to grace Greek features, it doesn't seem quite at home there.

Are you alright, she says. I'm sorry about Barbara, I should have warned you. We call her The Barbarian.

O I'm fine, I say, I've nothing against Barbara – not now, anyway – it's just…

What?

I'm feeling quite tired, Penelope. Do you think it would be OK if I had a bath?

A bath?

A bathe. Only I need towels to wipe myself, and I don't want to ask Barbara.

Of course! You silly girl. Of course you can have a bath. I'll get you a mountain of towels… Then she catches my face, grabs it in her hand, tilts my cheek to catch the light.

For a moment, I can't breathe at all. Neopolitan beauty, or Nemesis? – Which will she see?

You know, you've got really good bone structure there.

Have I? Really?

Yes – You could use a lot less foundation and it would show it off a whole lot better. Seriously, any Greek would kill for bones like yours.

She laughs.

What?

Nothing. It's just how we present our skin where I come from. Despite the fruit. The bath?

Leave it to me, she says. I'll fix it. And she does.

The Woman slips off the trousers of her trouser suit. Beneath, her legs are covered with ugly-looking blue-black blotches.

She's a stayer, Penelope, that much is obvious. Faithful and honest and true. Big bones, big heart. One of the noble Greeks. Even if her husband is a blasphemer. In another world, a future world, women like us might be friends. Look at all this she brought me! Soaps, perfumes, all the riches of Greece. My daughter would love them. Penny even warns me to lock the door, keep out the Barbarian.

O Let them come I say, if they don't mind bathing in the dark, they're welcome.

She drags a finger across the water – the bath is ready. She shakes the drops off her fingers.

Sounds like the banquet's starting upstairs. I thought I might go up later. Offer Clytaemnestra my help with Agamemnon. But I don't think she needs my help. Do you?

After all, this is Athens. Home of the heroic Greeks. A people without parallel, anywhere on earth.

As music drifts in, Nemesis removes her tunic; like her legs, her upper body is covered with ugly sores – the plague. She steps into the bath. She winces, then sits. A moment. As the lights fade, she cups the candle and blows it out.

Silence.

Blackout.

THE RETREATING WORLD

Character

ALI, an Iraqi man in his late twenties

The Retreating World was commissioned by the McCarter Theatre Center, Princeton NJ. The first performance took place at the Hotbed New Writing Festival, Cambridge in July 2002, with the following credits.

ALI, Hisham Matar

Directed by Patrick Morris

Designed by Idit Nathan

Menagerie's *Two Into War* production, which coupled *The Retreating World* with Fraser Grace's *Gifts of War*, was first produced at The Latchmere Theatre (Theatre 503), in March 2003, with the same personnel.

An Iraqi man, ALI, in his late twenties, enters. He is dressed casually, in slacks and a T-shirt. He is balancing a book on his head.

ALI: Nowadays you can pick up a book like this for next to nothing. Whole libraries, years and years of careful selection and loving looks, and maybe some reading, set out by the side of the road. For sale. For next to nothing. Unfortunately I bought this one before. Before. And it cost me. But it was worth it.

He tilts his head and lets the book drop on the stage.

Books can be used for many things besides reading.

He gives the book a couple of short, quick kicks.

For exercising the ankles and toes with short, controlled bursts of movement. Or

He snatches up the book.

a book can be used to create a man with a bookish face. It can be done.

He holds the book to hide his face for a moment.

I never had the knack for telling good jokes. The kind that slap your face and send your head spinning. My friend Samir Saboura, he could tell jokes. Once he told me a joke about rice pudding, two porcupines and a jockstrap; I laughed so hard I broke a tooth.

But this, this is a book on bird 'fancying' as they say in the north of England. It took me ages to understand even though I am fluent in English and have read Macaulay's speeches in order to really hear the English language. But this was not English. This was north of English and about pigeons and doves. Not stuff for the faint hearted.

It is a deadly serious book. One suspects, after fifty pages or so, that in fact it is not a book about keeping birds as a hobby, but something far more…important.

Like how to keep your lover, or swindle your friends. Or find inner peace.

But after one has negotiated, appreciated, and ingested the in's and out's of keeping pigeons, there are, considering the times – and you know what times we live in: whole libraries for sale, art books, leather bound in Baghdad in the thirties, obstetrics and radiology texts, copies of *British Medical Journals*. And something for you as well: first and second editions of *The Sun also Rises*. *Waiting for Godot*. And all for the price of a few cigarettes – considering the times there is only one real rule to keeping pigeons. And this rule, this golden rule is Not in this book: never name a pigeon after a member of your family or a dear friend. (*Beat*.) For two reasons: pigeons have short lives – and when a pigeon named after an uncle dies, this can be disconcerting. And second. These times are dangerous for pigeons: they can be caught and eaten…

And cannibalism can put you off a hobby.

I began collecting and trading pigeons and doves when I was fifteen. That was more than ten years ago, when birds clustered like flies in the palms along the avenues and my land was the land of dates. Do you remember that country? Back then, everyone could read and when my smallest dove developed a fever, I took her to the hospital, where there was free access to all health care facilities. Parents were fined for not sending their pigeons to school. The basic indicators that you use to measure the overall well-being of flying animals were some of the best in the world. And. And. (*Gently but firmly to himself.*) Shut up, Ali.

One of the birds I called Lak'aa Faseeh Zayer, after my grandmother. A real show off she was. This bird, known as a Feral Pigeon or Rock Dove, I bought off a trader

from North America: *Columba Livia*, in Latin. It has a
white rump and a double black wingbar. Now my
grandmother was tall and hard as a big stick and she
liked everything American. She drank her coffee from a
Campbell's Soup can. She worked as a maid in a hotel
wearing a set of trainers from a Sears Roebuck
Catalogue a cousin sent her from Wisconsin. I was
already a teenager when I got my first pigeon but when I
had trouble sleeping she would hold me in her arms and
sing to me. Her voice was like an old soft motor,
clinking and clanking. Much sweeter than any fruit:

He sings a short Arab lullaby his grandmother taught him.

She had only three teeth in front but she always said
song was not in the tooth but in the roof of the mouth,
where God lives. She was also a bit of a blasphemer.
Lak'aa Faseeh Zayer was her name. I would write her
name down for you but we have no pencils.

I became a student when I was seventeen. I had six birds
by then. I had one white-winged dove, also imported
from America. She I named Greta, after my little sister.
My father he loved movies and so my mother named my
sister Greta, after Garbo. We were secular, our family.
My birds, they were a mix of Christian, Jewish and
Muslim. They pulled out each other's feathers when they
got a chance, sometimes even a little blood but mostly
they got along well and crapped in the same pile. I won
third prize with Greta in 1989 at the International Bird
Show in Baghdad.

Books have other uses.

He stands on the book.

Now I am an inch and a half taller. (*He stands with one
foot off and one foot on.*) Now I am a crooked man, a
slanted man. Or to cut it short, for most of the world: an

Arab. And I have come here to speak to you about pigeons:

My favorite bird is the *Zenaida Macroura*, or Mourning Dove. Its name derives from its long, mournful, cooing call, which sounds something like this:

Makes a very impressive call of the mourning dove.

The mourning dove is a strong, fast flier that flushes up with a whirring of its wings. This first dove I bought, I named after my closest friend, Samir Saboura. We went to grade school together. While I drew birds, he made up words. He made up a word for the motion of a stone falling. (*Speaks a made-up word, with confidence.*) The way a fish flicks its tail in the water. (*Another word.*) The sound an apple makes when it's bit. (*Another word.*) Samir Saboura. A strong fast flier that flushed up with a whirring of his wings.

My Grandmother, Lak'aa Faseeh Zayer, took care of my pigeons when I was conscripted. Samir and I, we were in Saddam's army, not the elite Republican Guard, but just the ordinary shock troops. What luck. What luck that we managed to stay together throughout the war. We hid in bunkers for most of those weeks. Cursing Saddam when our captain was out. Cursing the Brits and the Yanks the rest of the time. And I missed my birds. But birds were prohibited in the bunkers. Prohibited. Prohibited by the laws of nations as were the fuel air explosive bombs, the napalm – Shhhh! – the cluster and anti-personnel weapons. Prohibited, as were the BLU-82 bombs, a 15,000 pound device – Shut up! – capable of incinerating every living thing, flying or grounded, within hundreds of yards... And me, I missed my birds. The way they looked at me, their eyes little pieces of peace sailing my way.

After the war, I sold them one by one, all twelve of
them. For food. For aspirin. I sold them. But not before I
sold the watch my Great Uncle gave me, the spoon my
Aunt gave Mother, with my name inscribed the day I
was born. Not before I sold my Shakespeare, in Arabic,
first, then my copies in English. Because I knew. I knew.
That my birds would not be shown at the next
convention.

I remember. I remember. Everything we say these days
begins with 'I remember'. Because the things we saved
from the past, we sell day by day for a future in a bucket
of slops and potato skins. A bunch of Dole bananas and a
bag of apples from Beirut cost a teacher's salary for a
month. Only the rich eat fruit. So all we can do is
remember. I remember, a few months after the bombing
stopped, my grandmother falling on a piece of broken
pipe, her thigh cut to the bone. Little pink pills. Little
pink pills of penicillin were all she needed. But these
were prohibited by the blockade, prohibited for import,
as are chemotherapy drugs and painkillers – Not again,
Ali! – (*Beat.*) Five thousand pigeons die a month because
of this blockade. No. (*Beat.*) Five thousand children die a
month because of this blockade… I will count to five
thousand and then perhaps you will see how many five
thousand is. (*Slowly.*) One, two, three, four, five, six,
seven, eight, nine, ten, eleven, twelve, thirteen, fourteen.
(*Beat.*) It takes a long time to count that far.

Little pink pills. That was all we needed to save Lak'aa
Faseeh Zayer, my grandmother. She lay in my mother's
arms, rotting from the waist down while the birds
disappeared from the avenues because the trees had died.
And this was the land of dates. How many dates? How
many birds? (*Slowly.*) One, two, three, four. The sadness
of numbers is that they do not stop and there is always
one more to follow. Just like birds.

Quotes.

> 'Do you ne'er think who made them, and who taught
> The dialect they speak, where melodies
> Alone are the interpreters of thought?'

'The Birds of Killingworth', Henry Wadsworth Longfellow. He was one of Samir's favorites, along with al-Mutanabi, al-Sayyab and Kanafani. And of course, the poets of love. (*Beat.*) And what of love? What is a book on the pigeon and the dove if it does not treat the philosophies of love? Is it in the dove that has been flying for miles and miles with hunger a sharp blue light across its breast, coming home, coming home? Is it in the woman's spine, rolling up and down, dice from the fire? Is it in the child's sleep, where death is a butterfly that rests on the finger, then away? I don't know. (*Beat.*) I don't know what love is. It goes. It comes. It goes. It comes. Samir Saboura. My friend. If love is in pieces, then he was a piece of love.

Tall, tall, he was. A handsome fellow with big dark eyes but, and I must say it, he walked like a pigeon. Now, pigeons are not really meant to walk. Their state of grace is to fly. But if they must walk, they walk like Samir walked. Like this:

He walks like Samir, bobbing his head in and out, taking sure but awkward steps.

It's possible his great grandfather was a flamingo. Samir. He was intelligent and hilarious, but he had one fault: he could hardly read. He was terribly dyslexic. So we would do the reading for him. Samir was always carrying a book, and whoever he came upon, he would say 'Read to me'. He'd memorize whole passages that he would recite at the most inopportune of moments. For instance, I had food poisoning when I was sixteen. All day I sat on the toilet, rocking and moaning. And, I must say it, stinking as well. But Samir would not leave my side. He would not leave me to suffer alone. Up and down the hallway outside the bathroom he strode, reciting pieces of Hart Crane. While I sputtered and farted in agony, snatches of The Bridge sailed in and out of my consciousness and kept me from despair:

He quotes Samir reciting Hart Crane.

> 'And if they take your sleep away sometimes
> They give it back again. Soft sleeves of sound
> attend the darkling harbour, the pillowed bay.'

A good friend, Samir. He had a library that even his teachers envied. He couldn't read the books himself, but he slept and ate among them. Running his big hands over their spines, he would grin at us: 'I cannot read them, but I can touch them.' He was so intimate with his books that he could close his eyes and find a book by its smell.

He tears a small piece of paper from a book and smells it, then eats it.

Books can also, in extreme times, be used as sustenance. But such eating makes for a parched throat. Many mornings I wake and I am thirsty. I turn on the taps but there is no running water. A once-modern city of three million people, with no running water for years now. The toilets are dry because we have no sanitation. Sewage pools in the streets. When we wish to relieve ourselves, we squat beside the dogs. At night, we turn on the lights to read the books we have forgotten we have sold, but there is no electricity. We go to the cupboard to eat cold cans of soup but there is no food processing so the cupboards are bare. A couple of us wanted to write a few polite words of complaint to the United Nations Sanctions Committee, but it has blocked the import of pencils as it is feared they might be used for making 'weapons of mass destruction'. Just recently it was reported that despite the blockade, at the very tops of some of the most remote mosques, nests have been found made entirely of pencils. (*Whispers.*) Stockpiling.

He opens the book again.

Sometimes, if the occasion is right, a book is for reading.

He snaps the book shut. Then recites quietly.

> 'Some say the world will end in fire,
> Some say ice.
> From what I've tasted of desire,
> I hold with those who favor fire.'

Robert Frost. You teach that in school. 88,500 tons of bombs. Write this down without pencils: the equivalent of seven and a half atomic bombs of the size that incinerated Hiroshima. 900 tons of radioactive waste spread over much of what was once the land of dates. (*He gets rid of the book.*) Somewhere within this information is a lullaby.

Sings a piece of the Arab lullaby that he sung before. Beat.

And this, my friends, is documented. Fact. Fact. By the European Parliament, 1991. Members of the committee recorded the testimony, drinking cups of cold coffee: the defeated troops were surrendering. We, a nation of 'unpeople', were surrendering. Samir and myself, along side seven hundred other men. We were dirty and tired and hungry, sucking orange mints because the napalm made our gums bleed. That morning, I'd relieved myself beside the others while invisible jets broke the black glass sky across the horizon. My friend Samir did the same. And then we walked towards the American unit to surrender, our arms raised beside seven hundred other men. Samir, he said to me – this is not documented – He said: I want to put my hands in a bucket of cold water.

Shut up, I said, keep your hands up. Samir said, I want to smell the back of my father's neck. Shut up, I said. Shut up. We're almost home. Samir Saboura said 'I want to tell an astonishing joke until you cry for relief'.

As we walked towards them – This is documented – the commander of the US unit fired, at one man, an anti-tank missile. A missile meant to pierce armour. At one man. The rest of us, arms still raised, stopped walking. I remember. I remember. I could not. I could not recognize. My friend Samir. A piece of his spine stuck upright in the sand. His left hand blown so high in the air it was still falling. Then they opened fired on the rest of us.

A bullet hit me in the back as I ran. Out of hundreds, thousands in that week, a handful of us survived. I lived. (*Beat*.) Funny. That I am still here. The dead are dead. The living, we are the ghosts. We no longer say goodbye to one another. With the pencils we do not have we write our names so the future will know we were here. So that the past will know we are coming.

He quotes.

> 'In a world that seems so very puzzling is it any wonder birds have such appeal? Birds are, perhaps, the most eloquent expression of reality.'

Roger Tory Peterson, American Ornithologist, born 1908.

He quotes again.

> 'War is hell.'

Pete Williams, Defense department spokesman, on confirming that US army earth movers buried alive, in their trenches, up to 8,000 Iraqi soldiers. (*Beat*.) Yep. Yep.

War is hell. And birds are perhaps the most eloquent expression of reality. In Arabic we say:

Says in Arabic, twice, the equivalent of 'fuck that'.

Which is the equivalent of: 'fuck that'.

I sold my last bird a few days ago. Tomorrow I will sell the cage. The day after that I will have nothing more to sell. But I keep track of the buyers, and who the buyers sell to. I go to their homes and I ask for the bones. Usually the family is kind, or frightened of me, and they give me the bones after the meal. I boil the bones and keep them in a bucket.

We now notice an old steel bucket that is elsewhere on stage. He takes the bucket.

Listen.

He shakes the bucket. We hear the sound of bones rattling, though the sound comes not from his bucket but from all around us.

It is a kind of music.

He holds the bucket out to the audience.

These are the bones of those who have died, from the avenue of palms, from the land of dates. I have come here to give them to you for safekeeping. (*Beat.*) Catch them. If you can.

He roughly throws the contents of the bucket at the audience. Instead of bones, into the air and across the audience spills hundreds of white feathers.

the end

BUTTERFLY FINGERS

Characters

TERRI, a blonde, British, woman

MARTIN, an American serviceman

Time: present
Place: a US army base somewhere in America

Butterfly Fingers was first produced by Soho Theatre as part of a play-in-a-day event, Write Now, in November 2003. The commission was to write, rehearse and produce a short play in 24 hours, based on the day's news.

It was directed by Janette Smith, and performed by the following cast:

TERRI, Candida Benson

MARTIN, Darren Strange

The play was revised in 2004 for the Hotbed Festival, Cambridge, directed by Josie Rourke, and designed by Lucy Osborne. The performers were:

TERRI, Anna Maxwell-Martin

MARTIN, John Kirk

I

A bar in the officers' mess at a US air base. TERRI and MARTIN enter already in conversation, and approach a table. MARTIN is wearing US Army uniform, and carries a clipboard.

MARTIN: So – you are a blonde, right?

TERRI: A what?

MARTIN: A blonde – your hair, your hair-colour, that's what they call a blonde hair tone? Am I right?

TERRI: I suppose so.

MARTIN: Naturally blonde?

TERRI: Ash blonde.

MARTIN: Sorry. Can I ask…is the hair blonde in actuality, or is there some other colour under that?

TERRI: Is this really relevant, Lieutenant?

MARTIN: It's required, Ms Baxter.

TERRI: Required in actuality.

Beat.

MARTIN: Why don't we startover. You wanna go some place else?

TERRI: No, no, this is fine. Thankyou. Thankyou for the drink.

MARTIN: My pleasure, Ms Baxter.

TERRI: It's nice here. Informal.

They exchange a smile – chemistry is in the air.

MARTIN: OK. Hair Colour: Tick A Blonde, B Red, C Other.

TERRI: Brunette?

MARTIN: No brunette.
Are you saying your hair is brunette in actuality?

TERRI: I think I'm saying it's Other.

MARTIN: It looks blonde.

TERRI: It is blonde…today.

MARTIN: OK. I'm gonna make a note of that.
'The applicant is an Unnaturally Blonde Woman…'

TERRI: Lieutenant!
I sound like a freak.

MARTIN: Artificially blonde?

TERRI: Blonde – by choice.

MARTIN: That's good. That's positive. We're making progress, Ms Baxter.

TERRI: Good. I'm glad. So, have you finished your questions now?

MARTIN: Not by a long way Ms Baxter. May I call you Charlie?

TERRI: Terri. The name's Terri.

MARTIN: I'm sorry, that's an error. There's a process we have to observe here Terri – we just have to plough right on through. Is that OK with you?

TERRI: That's fine.

MARTIN: You sure now?

TERRI: Absolutely.

MARTIN: OK, next section – age.
I'm gonna come back to age.
Build. Now, I would describe you as slender. Is that accurate?

TERRI: Do you mean naturally?

MARTIN: It's best we try not to be too hostile at this point Ms Baxter. You want I should enter you as Slim?

TERRI: No, Slender's fine.

Beat.

Thankyou.

MARTIN: It's a pleasure Miss Baxter.
So is there a reason you're blonde by choice?

TERRI: What?

MARTIN: Is there a reason you choose to be blonde instead of Other?

TERRI: Because I like it…?

MARTIN: Sure. And Gentlemen prefer blondes, too, right. Directors, and so on. Public, too I guess.

TERRI: Aren't you forgetting someone?

MARTIN: Right. The Camera.

TERRI: Some of the choices I make really are for myself. Lots of women feel the same. Lighter, Brighter. 'You have more fun when you're blonde.'

MARTIN: Well. I can understand that.

TERRI: Also my lovers prefer blonde. I'm more fun then, too.

Beat.

MARTIN: Ms Baxter's build is…slim, slender and mouthwateringly attractive.

TERRI: What was that?

MARTIN: You have a problem with my noting you as attractive?

TERRI: Lieutenant, I think I have a problem with 'mouthwatering'.

Beat.

MARTIN: I don't think you need have Ms Baxter.

Beat.

TERRI: My image is not just about the way I look, is it, Lieutenant. It's also about the way I regard myself, the way I behave, don't you think?

MARTIN: Humility. Good point. OK I'm gonna consolidate this… So… Miss Baxter is a tall, slender and moderately attractive woman…

TERRI: Plain attractive. That's better – for American ears. I would have thought.

MARTIN: Does that work for you? Plain attractive?

TERRI: What do you suggest. Ugly attractive?

MARTIN: How about I put 'pleasantly attractive'.

TERRI: Fine. Thankyou.
Undeniably attractive, would be better (still).

MARTIN: Undeniably attractive. That's good. Puts the onus right back on the viewer. See that's why we come to people like you, Miss Baxter, you have a firm grip on image, and great command of the English Language

TERRI: 'People like me'? Are you considering other people for this post?

MARTIN: I let that slip out Ms Baxter. Can we take a raincheck on the answer just now? No pun intended. Now, if we can just…

TERRI: You're talking to NBC, aren't you?
Charlie Whiston.

MARTIN: We are having a preliminary discussion with Ms Whiston. Precautionary. Case things don't work out.

TERRI: Do I strike you as a woman who doesn't work out, Lieutenant?

MARTIN: I'll be frank Ms Baxter – for this duty, I don't see a reason any sane man would look further than what I see before me in the mess today.

Beat.

TERRI: Thankyou. That's very nice of you.

MARTIN: It's just – I got orders, thass all.
You want me to continue, Terri?

TERRI: Fine.

MARTIN: OK – Eyes.

TERRI: Eyes. Yes. Two. Two eyes, both functioning. Can we move onto something beyond externals, please.

MARTIN: Eye *colour* is the focus here… Hey now, don't you cry Ms Baxter.

TERRI: I'm sorry. Not very professional. I've just had my heart set on this. If we are going to go to war again, I want to play my part, does that sound silly?

MARTIN: No, not at all, Miss Baxter. That…that's patriotic.

Beat.

You know what Miss Baxter? To hell with this.

TERRI: You're giving up on me, are you

MARTIN: No ma'am, no, I… I have to be honest Ms Baxter. There's Process, and there's Say-So. My say-so has quite an influence round here.

TERRI: Really?

MARTIN: Yes ma'am. I am quite a high ranking officer, I rank pretty high upstairs.

TERRI: Well. Maybe you could put a word in for me, upstairs.

MARTIN: Yes ma'am, I intend to.

TERRI: That's very kind.

Pause.

MARTIN: Would you do me that thing Ms Baxter? You know what I'm talking about? You stand in front there, kinda side on, and you do that move with your hand.

TERRI: That move?

MARTIN: You know the thing Ms Baxter. You draw your hands down the coast there…

TERRI: What here? In front of everyone.

MARTIN: C'mon Terri – who's looking? Only me.

TERRI: Alright. Like this, you mean?

MARTIN: Woah-woah. That's it. Slower.

TERRI: This?

MARTIN: Say the words, could you?

TERRI: Er…there's a warm front blowing in from the North tonight…

MARTIN: Again – just the hand, this time, real slow… O God. I tell you Miss Baxter, you knew how many of our boys you touch with that hand.

TERRI: Now you're humouring me.

MARTIN: No really. It's all they say. That's why you're here. Sea crew, marines, all the same. Terri Baxter's Weather Time from the East Coast Network – tune in, turn on. You're pretty big with the boys in the field.

TERRI: I'm pleased to hear it.

MARTIN: Seriously you are massively big with the forces out there.

TERRI: Good.

Beat.

MARTIN: Truth is Miss Baxter… I'm pretty massive for you myself. Right now.

Beat.

I shouldn't have said that.

TERRI: No, I don't think you should.

MARTIN: Forgive me.

TERRI: Forgiven. I don't mix business with pleasure, that's all, Lieutenant.

MARTIN: Martin.

TERRI: Martin.

MARTIN: That's a good rule Ms Baxter. Bout business and…

MARTIN gulps hard. Pause.

Far as business is concerned, we're pretty much done with business fer the day.

TERRI: Really.

MARTIN: Yes ma'am. We're right through to plain old service time.

TERRI: Service time? What on earth's that?

MARTIN: Juss...down time, basically. Lotta guys get home to their wives about now. Base gets deserted. Usually I use this time for pleasure. Leisure. I have this...room upstairs.

Pause.

TERRI: This wouldn't be the Lieutenant's idea of the casting couch, would it?

MARTIN: No ma'am. Not at all, no, not ever.

Pause.

There's no couch in there anyway. We have a table, I sometimes shove that up against a wall.

TERRI: Don't tell me: you can tell a lot about a person by their hands.

She has put her hand upon his shoulder, or knee. He smiles. She smiles too.

Do you know what I think Martin? I think you it's time we saw exactly how massive you are....

Lights.

II

TERRI, drink in hand, is sitting on the table, reading and editing the application they have cobbled together. MARTIN is the cat who got the cream.

TERRI: …in conclusion. Ms Baxter is a media-conversant and extremely lens-friendly professional. She is energetic, self-possessed, and has the proven – has the *undeniable* – ability to capture men's hearts. Great in spirit herself, Terri certainly inspires greatness in her fellow men.
Well, I think we've proved that point.

MARTIN: Yes ma'am.

TERRI: Last, and most important of all, Ms Baxter's gift for weather control will be vital to a successful campaign, making her the ideal Face of War for the forthcoming conflict.

MARTIN: Whoa whoa – what's that? A 'gift for weather control'? Kinda strong don't you think.

TERRI: O? I thought we'd covered that. Terri's hands flutter, and the earth moves.

MARTIN: We're talking about upstairs. Right?

Beat.

Are you seriously saying you control the weather, Terri?

Beat.

TERRI: Would that be a problem?

MARTIN: A problem? Hell yes. We have a large program already working on weather control, we're talking billions of dollars of investment here…!

TERRI: Pathetic. Absolutely pathetic.

I wave my hands for a living, Martin. I smile, I stand sideways in front of a blue screen – You really think that I think I control the weather?

MARTIN: No. No, of course not...

TERRI: Good.

It's minds I do control, obviously.

MARTIN: I'm sorry...?

TERRI: Well that is my purpose, isn't it? That is what this post is all about?

MARTIN: Pardon me? Mind control...?

TERRI: What is the attraction of Terri Baxter for the military? The accent? My innate intelligence...?

MARTIN: The accent's kinda cute...

TERRI: ... The hand thing?

The hand thing. Always the fucking hands. God I hate this business...

MARTIN: Tell me about weather control Terri. If you do not control the weather, why are you putting weather control on the application? Why are you talking now about mind control?

Beat.

TERRI: You're a high ranking officer. Surely you know the answer? A butterfly flaps its wings on our continent, and somewhere, far away...

MARTIN: Right. This is one of those hippy things.

TERRI: Not a hippy thing. It's a respectable scientific theory. Chaos theory. You're a military man, surely you know about chaos.

MARTIN: We – try to keep Chaos out of the military Ms Baxter.

Beat.

TERRI: The point is, Martin, I'm a butterfly. I live at the butterfly end of life's equation. That's why you people need me. Isn't it?

MARTIN: The what end of what, exactly?

TERRI: A butterfly flaps its wings, and, half a world away – there's a storm. And I am aware of that. And I…play my part.
When the West goes to war, naturally there's a storm, but that's OK, because I'm there. I say 'rain', and a million people – probably nearer ten million, in fact, all over the East Coast – think 'raindrops'. I say, 'sunny spells'; in a million mind's eyes the sun pokes its warm syrupy fingers through a scary looking cloud. I whisper 'breeze', there's a child's breath, my own breath on my daughter's neck. Little hairs soft as breath itself. That's the kind of weather control you really need. And I deliver that. For the next year I'll be doing features on army wives waving their husbands off. Women, who serve alongside men, reports explaining how difficult it is keep your hair groomed in the desert. I keep the world's eyes firmly on the butterfly, away from the tornado.
That's right, isn't it. That is how it works.

MARTIN: Terri – if that's how you feel – why, in God's name, do you want this post?

TERRI: Because I'm a weather girl. A stupid dumb blonde woman, tired of standing sideways. Haven't you heard, I can do a thing with my hands that drives men wild.

Beat.

Well it's dirty work but someone has to do it.

Beat.

O my God. You'd rather I didn't realize.
You really do want a dumb blonde don't you…

MARTIN: Terri, how do you expect to do this job if you're not dumb?

TERRI: It's a deal, Martin. I'm a professional.

MARTIN: And you're happy with that deal?.

TERRI: Not happy exactly, no…

MARTIN: Then what? What are you doing here Terri?

TERRI: I'm doing what has to be done.
We all do. We all do it, there's no need to look shocked, we're all taking the king's shilling every day of our lives…

MARTIN: 'The king's shilling' – what is that?

TERRI: Never mind. I'm just saying, there's what we see in front of us, and there's the other thing. And we focus on what's close.

Beat

MARTIN: You know what, you need to grow up Terri . Seriously.

TERRI: I beg your pardon?

MARTIN: Be mature. Take responsibility for what you think. If that's what you believe goes on, and you believe something else is true, say it.

TERRI: O right. Sure.

MARTIN: Why not?

TERRI: Because it's not what I'm for.

MARTIN: Forget the job Terri. We're talking about you now. About Terri. Alright?

TERRI: Alright.

MARTIN: Why not here? Now? Go ahead, say it the way you see it for once. Forget mind control, forget your damn butterfly metaphors, let it out. Get it off your beautiful chest, say it. Tell the truth according to Terri Baxter.

TERRI: And what would that gain me? Won't change anything. Doesn't pay the rent. Doesn't save anyone. Doesn't get me out of East Coast fucking network TV either, does it? Well does it?

MARTIN: Terri listen to me. I met a woman today. A beautiful, exceptional woman. She's smart. She's a woman who has to say, what she has to say. She may not get another chance. If she takes this job, and we both know she has it by the balls, that's it for Terri Baxter; free speech – forget that. Free speech out, script in, autocue. For all I know she may not even get to do the hands anymore.

TERRI: You mean I won't get the chance to turn you on again?

MARTIN: Save your beautiful, limpid soul, Terri. I'm begging you, don't take the fucking job. OK. Take the job, but say it now. For me. Once. Think of the butterfly, Terri.
Who knows what happens if your soul flaps its wings just once. What effect that may have, for people the other side of the world, for the future, for a guy like me. For your daughter, Terri.

Beat.

TERRI: O that's very clever. Very good.

MARTIN: Not 'clever' Terri. Honest.

TERRI: Honest? What do you know about being honest?

MARTIN: Honest with yourself.
Can you look yourself in the face and say I know what I see, and I've said it. Just that one time. When I was free.

Pause. TERRI swallows hard, and does her stuff.

TERRI: A light wind will blow in from the west.

MARTIN: Louder Terri.

TERRI: A light wind will blow in from the west. Heavy showers sweep down from the north. Storms are possible, at sea. For some of us tonight, just off our map, the air will catch fire, melt children, strangers become ash. In the morning, deserts will be larger. Deeper. Thick with the down from people's eyelids. Innocence will be gone. Eyes that see our terror will be always knowing, always seeing, all gone.
But nearer home, a much calmer picture as we approach the weekend. And I'll be back with you, again, the same time, tomorrow night, on East Coast Network TV...
There. How was that?

Beat. She has lost the job.

Shit.

MARTIN: You know what? I had it on good authority you were completely fucking shallow. Interviews over, Terri, the flapping starts here.

TERRI: And that's all it takes? A little honesty, a dumb blonde to make a few honest connections?

MARTIN: Well, you know what they say Terri. Honesty is next to chaos. But hey – thanks fer stopping by. I had a good time today. Really.

TERRI: Well. me too.

Oh come on Martin, don't be such a prude. You can't make people stare at the tornado. They're not stupid. People get less stupid every day. You're going to need my butterfly fingers, even more this time, don't you think?

Martin?

MARTIN: Don't worry about us Ms Baxter. My guess is, we'll do what we always do. Stick to plan A. We'll go with Charlie.

Lights.

The End.

A STATE OF INNOCENCE

Characters

UM HISHAM QISHTA, Palestinian woman,
early fifties, from Rafah

YUVAL, Israeli soldier, twenty-seven, from Tel Aviv

SHLOMO, Israeli architect, elegant man, fifties

Place: Something like a small zoo, but more silent, empty, in
Rafah, Palestine.

Time: Now

Set: An almost bare stage, perhaps a few disjointed pieces to
make the merest suggestion of a zoo. Or a space that once
dreamed it was a zoo.

7:84 Theatre Company (Scotland) commissioned *A State of Innocence* in 2004. It was first performed at Theatre 503, the Latchmere Pub, on 19 April 2005, with the following cast:

YUVAL, Conrad Westmaas

UM HISHAM, Eve Polycarpou

SHLOMO, Richard Hollis

Directed by Raz Shaw

YUVAL stands center stage, dressed as a zookeeper might be dressed, but carrying an Uzi, but casually, as though it were not there. UM HISHAM stands nearby watching him. He is at first not aware of her and speaks to the public.

YUVAL: I say to him when we're alone, I say: 'He whom love touches not, walks in darkness.' Do you, my friend? Do you walk in darkness? And then he winks at me. Ever had a porcupine wink at you? It's like the whole symposiums in that flick of a gesture. He knows. Damn it, he knows! And his name is Shadack Winko. An it's a small zoo too, but it's got a big spirit, and only two emus: Tricky Beak and Horton. Tricky Beak only has one eye and her beak's twisted. Her brother is Horton. Horton is…dull. Two camels. Dromedary. One's named Fairway and the other is Hoboken Bromwell. Then two ring tailed cats, Buddy and Briggs. Three water buffalo, Chesterfield, Erkle and Alfalfa. And one puny monkey: Dingleberry Dibbit. And damn it, yes, I named every one of them. And my name is Yuval. I'm a grad student in philosophy from Tel Aviv University. My folks came over from New York when they were kids. And we go back to the Big Apple every summer and visit family. But I grew up in the shopping centers and apartment complexes of the middle class suburbs of Tel Aviv.

UM HISHAM has begun to softly sing a song in Arabic as he speaks.

But every morning I wake and an animal… No. But it's true. A different piece. It's back the next morning but then another part is gone again. There is something I don't know.

Speaks in Hebrew: 'Something is wrong with this zoo. God help us.' UM HISHAM's song can now clearly be heard.

Excuse me but that's against the rules.

UM HISHAM: What is?

YUVAL: Gurgling.

UM HISHAM: I'm not gurgling. I'm singing.

YUVAL: Gurgling. Singing. Same thing. Not allowed in this zoo. Only the animals may sing and gurgle. It's their home after all. Would you like to see Shadack Winko? He's napping but I can wake him for you. Didn't you bring your family to the zoo with you, or are you a selfish woman?

UM HISHAM: Rafah.

YUVAL: I've been to Rafah. I don't discriminate. Everyone is welcome in my tiny zoo. But remember that 'the one who comes to kill us, we shall rise early and kill him'. All animals here – excepting perhaps Twisty Beak – are morally justified and necessary to our survival. We're always under attack. I'm not afraid of you. Are you a terrorist?

UM HISHAM: Palestinorist. Terrestinian. Palerrorist. I was born in the country of Terrorist. I commit terrible acts of Palestinianism. I eat liberty from a bowl on the Wall. Fanatic. Security. Democracy.

YUVAL: (*Interrupts.*) Don't get playful with me. You want to throw me in the sea.

UM HISHAM: I just might. But I can't get to the sea. Seventeen and a half checkpoints keep me from it. You don't have tortoises. Why don't you have tortoises?

YUVAL: I'm twenty-seven years old.

UM HISHAM: Where is the ostrich?

YUVAL: I studied two semesters at Oxford.

UM HISHAM: Where is the kangaroo?

YUVAL: (*Says in Hebrew.*) Rafah is a cesspool. Your mind is sick.

UM HISHAM: Yes. Rafah is a cesspool and my mind is sick.

YUVAL: You understand Hebrew?

UM HISHAM: How is your mother?

YUVAL: She doesn't like the zoo.

UM HISHAM: I've got something that belongs to her.

YUVAL: (*Laughs.*) I don't think so, Lady.

UM HISHAM: I came to this zoo a couple years ago. There was a small swimming pool.

She looks for the place where the pool was on stage, then finds it.

Yes. It was here. I brought my daughter Asma here to swim.

YUVAL: There is no swimming pool here. Did you get a ticket when you came in?

UM HISHAM finds another spot on the stage.

UM HISHAM: There were two slides here, near the bird aviary.

YUVAL: How do you know my mother?

UM HISHAM: I know it's hard to believe, looking at it now, but it was beautiful here.

SHLOMO, a man of about fifty years of age, ambles onto the stage carrying a clipboard and a wooden box for carrying his surveying equipment. He looks a little confused at his surroundings but then shrugs in acceptance. He puts the box down and begins to make notes. He gestures at YUVAL.

SHLOMO: You. You in charge here?

YUVAL: Yes, sir.

SHLOMO: This place is full of holes. A veritable security cluster-fuck as we say in the business.

YUVAL: What business?

SHLOMO: Anyone else here? Just the two of you then. (*Makes notes.*) Nothing more sacred. Mother and son. Like the land and the settler – though the ones from Brooklyn …don't get me started!

UM HISHAM: He is not –

YUVAL: She is not –

SHLOMO: An architect. But I am. And an architect is naturally a philosopher, (*To YUVAL.*) as you wish to be. And this zoo…is a disgrace to zionist architecture.

UM HISHAM: All Israeli building in the occupied territories since 1948 is zionist. All demolitions also. My first house in 1967 –

SHLOMO chants loudly in order to drown out UM HISHAM.

SHLOMO: Homa Umigdal! Homa Umigdal! Homa Umigdal!

YUVAL: He's mad.

SHLOMO: Homa Umigdal. Was your house part of a wall and tower model?

UM HISHAM: No.

SHLOMO: I thought not.

He proceeds to help UM HISHAM onto the wooden box. He then links arms with YUVAL, forming a 'wall' around her 'tower'.

The wall and tower model, the Homa Umigdal, is the cradle of the nation, the very nest and egg that made the desert bloom. Circle the wagons, up with the periscope! Homa Umigdal – a prayer, a rhyme. And a spell.

He and YUVAL rotate around UM HISHAM. SHLOMO gets YUVAL to chant softly: 'Homa Umigdal, Homa Umigdal, Homa Umigdal.' Then he stops the chants.

Shhh. So, my good woman, what do you see?

UM HISHAM: Palestinians.

SHLOMO: Exactly! And we are?

UM HISHAM: Lunatics.

SHLOMO: (*Stopping the 'dance'.*) Protection. Homa Umigdal.

UM HISHAM: The model was a machine of invasion.

YUVAL: Yeah. I read about it at Oxford.

SHLOMO: Anti-semites, there. All of them. Homa Umigdal. Since we cannot remove this zoo –

UM HISHAM: You can't remove this zoo. It's a ruin.

SHLOMO: I've made my living building on ruins. As I say, since we cannot remove this zoo to a hilltop, which is where one is truly safe, we shall have to squeeze it into the homa umigdal model.

UM HISHAM: And the animals?

SHLOMO: They will feel safer. Happier. The fear of a terrorist attack can put an animal off its food. Bad for business. I will propose to the government that each animal have a wall and tower.

YUVAL: Ever seen the penguin pool at London Zoo? Now that's archit–

SHLOMO: Exactly! But higher walls and a real tower.

YUVAL: But I read that the concrete walkway was hard on their feet.

SHLOMO: Security has its price.

UM HISHAM: How will visitors see the penguins?

SHLOMO: Ah, but the penguins will be able to see the visitors, which is far more important.

YUVAL: We don't have any penguins. Can you do the Homa umigdal for the porcupine?

SHLOMO: Of course. I'm an architect!

UM HISHAM: Where are the tortoises?

SHLOMO: Homa Umigdal!

UM HISHAM: Where is the Ostrich?

SHLOMO: Homa Umigdal!

UM HISHAM: Where is the kangaroo?

YUVAL: How the hell should he know? I went to sleep on duty one afternoon and I woke up in this (*Curses in Hebrew.*) zoo. Have you seen the animals in the morning? They scream all night. I run from cage to cage but it's nothing but darkness inside. But the screams. The camels are the worst. (*Makes the sound of a camel scream.*) And in the morning I find pieces in the cages. Pieces of themselves. The emus are missing their toes. The ring tailed cats have no tails. The water buffalo. Their long ribs have fallen out of their bodies so their sides have collapsed. And the monkey. I cannot speak of the monkey.

SHLOMO: I saw the monkey on my way in. He looked just fine.

YUVAL: But that's just it. By the afternoon the pieces have grown back, only to be torn away again each night.

SHLOMO: Now you are being dramatic.

UM HISHAM: It's true. I've seen it.

SHLOMO: Bauhaus. Big deal.

YUVAL: (*In Hebrew, panicked.*) Oh my God. Oh my God. Oh my God.

SHLOMO slaps YUVAL in the face to bring him 'round.

SHLOMO: Snap out of it. Lets talk about Tel Aviv? huh?

YUVAL: Alright, alright. From the Book of Ezekiel.

SHLOMO: And?

UM HISHAM: He doesn't know.

SHLOMO: Very likely the only city to be named after a book, Herzl's futuristic, and –

UM HISHAM: (*Finishes his sentence.*) – not very good, novel *Altneuland.* First published 1904 and translated as –

YUVAL: *Tel Aviv.*

SHLOMO: Yes. What useless facts we architects acquire.

UM HISHAM: Better than collecting facts on the ground: your illegal settlements.

SHLOMO: Your mother sounds like –

YUVAL: She's not –

UM HISHAM: I'm not –

SHLOMO: (*Suddenly quotes, excited.*) 'Move, run and grab as many hilltops as you can to enlarge the Jewish settlements because everything we take now will stay ours...everything we don't grab will go to them.'

YUVAL: Ariel Sharon. Before he was Prime –

SHLOMO: That's right. But I am not like that over-ripe tic of a man. I do not confuse a hilltop with holiness.

UM HISHAM: I am a Palestinian. I am not his mother.

SHLOMO: Oh.

UM HISHAM: You with your building, building. All these red-roofed houses on the hills and around Al-Quds so our land is cut up into tiny useless slices. Homa Umigdal. Your houses watch our every move. They suck up our water, ruin our groves. And when they are full, they shit on us. You are a butcher not an architect. You eat up our future.

YUVAL: And given the chance you would eat us.

SHLOMO: I do not eat anymore. I will be 96 years old in November.

YUVAL: What? You look barely forty.

UM HISHAM: The lies of an Israeli architect!

SHLOMO: I assure you I am indeed that old. I bathe in the Dead Sea. Each time I give it some of my dying.

UM HISHAM: You are a funny man and at moments I am entertained. But I don't have time for you today. Leave us alone. Take your wall and tower with you.

YUVAL: She's right. This is no place for you. You give me chills.

SHLOMO: But I must redesign the zoo. And…and I am lonely. I have traveled so far. Ninety-six years! I was a Red Guard, a proud soviet until the revolution began to eat its own. I was lucky to escape with my life. But the zealous survive! I was a zealous revolutionary, then a zealous agricultural expert in Birobidzhan, Siberia, an autonomous republic for Jewish farmers. A paradise compared to this mess, I can tell you. Except the winters were hellish. And now I am a zealous architect. I might just turn around and become a zealous socialist again. It is possible. I am related to that bastard Kaganovich, the last Jewish Stalinist until Khruschev kicked him in the teeth. So, is there hope for me?

UM HISHAM: Hope? What is hope? My daughter Asma liked the turtles best.

SHLOMO: Christ I'm hungry.

UM HISHAM: Of course you are. So buck up. There's a fresh ruin in the Saladin district of Rafah. (*Breathes.*) Can you smell the dust in the air?

SHLOMO: (*Breathes too.*) Yes. Yes I can smell it. The crumble of walls. The smell of crushed linen. Toys bursting like fruit beneath the dozer's blade. Where in Saladin?

UM HISHAM: Second street from the left, number five. There were pigeons on the roof. Six of them.

SHLOMO: How many rooms in the house?

UM HISHAM: Four rooms. Large ones.

SHLOMO: Delicious.

SHLOMO exits excitedly.

UM HISHAM: And the walls in the bathroom were blue. In the hall there were orange birds on the tiles on the floor.

YUVAL: Yes. Orange birds on the floor. That's my mother's house.

UM HISHAM: And the ceiling was yellow.

YUVAL: No. The ceiling in my mother's house is white. And on the wall the tiles are

YUVAL/UM HISHAM: Blue Flowers with pink leaves.

YUVAL: How do you know this? What the fuck are you saying? I know that hallway. I know it like the back of my hand.

UM HISHAM: Yes. You have beautiful hands. But do you know your own hands? What do they do while you sleep?

YUVAL: (*Playful.*) Uh oh. Are you getting nasty on me?

UM HISHAM: Weeks ago. Your forefinger pressed the starter on your brand new Merkava tank.

YUVAL: Merkava. Baddest bad-assed tank to ever float the desert. Have you heard the stereo systems on those mother fuckers? It's like a concert you can hear from the moon.

YUVAL screams a couple lines of rock and roll, but just the tune, not words. Then quits abruptly and stares at UM HISHAM. Suddenly she does the rock and roll line back to him, but even better. Then she stares back.

UM HISHAM: And with five other tanks and two bulldozers you met the tortoises.

YUVAL: So this is about the damn turtles?

UM HISHAM: Yes. It begins with the turtles. In the zoo. The tiny zoo in Al-Brazil, Rafah. In Gaza. The turtles lined up to defend the zoo. They say their armor was aglow in the dusty light. That you could see it for miles. But your treds are four feet wide. A turtle weighs a pound and a half. The Merkava tank weighs sixty tons.

YUVAL: Sixty-five tons. Fully loaded. The new fire control system developed by El Op includes advanced features with the capability to acquire and lock onto moving targets.

UM HISHAM: Turtles are moving targets.

YUVAL: The Merkava 4 is powered by a GD 883 v-12 Diesel Engine rated at 1,500 hp.

YUVAL / UM HISHAM: (*Speaking together.*) The new engine represents a 25 per cent increase in power…

YUVAL: …compared to the 1,200 hp powerpack

UM HISHAM: (*Finishes for him.*) installed on the Merkava 3. Weight: sixty-five tons, fully loaded, as you say. A turtle a pound and a half. It was a quick death for the turtles. Then you and your buddies crushed the rest of the zoo. The ostrich was flattened, as were the squirrels, goats and kangaroos. The single deer lay on her side all night, paddling with her broken legs as though she were swimming.

YUVAL: Hey. The military dismissed those accusations. A spokesman said the soldiers released the animals from their cages in a compassionate gesture to prevent them being harmed.

UM HISHAM: Why the zoo? The only place for children to go to touch animals and hear their sounds.

YUVAL: I told you why. Because gurgling is no longer permitted. There was gurgling coming from the Rafah zoo, day in, day out. Gurgle, gurgle, gurgle. The children were gurgling.

UM HISHAM: Not gurgling. Singing.

YUVAL: Same thing.

UM HISHAM: No. It's not.

YUVAL: I'm not a bad soldier.

UM HISHAM: You never killed a human being. Though perhaps, sooner or later.

YUVAL: In my dreams I hear the animals screaming. Plato said 'If there were only some way of contriving that a state or an army should be made up of lovers, they would be the very best governors of their own city.'

UM HISHAM: Perhaps. But not of ours.

YUVAL: I'm sorry about the zoo.

UM HISHAM: The zoo is gone.

YUVAL: No. We're here right now.

UM HISHAM: You never wanted to be a soldier, Yuval.

YUVAL: Don't be foolish. If it weren't for the state of Israel, I would not exist. The IDF is a page torn from the book of God. And the IDF is not only the Israeli Defense Force but Ideology Defined as Freedom. What do you think I am, stupid? Do you really think that I believe that the Palestinian is a –

UM HISHAM: – land-grabbing trickster with a head full of gasoline-soaked rags, feeding off

YUVAL: the pure, steamed and distilled –

UM HISHAM / YUVAL: – hatred of Jews?

UM HISHAM: Do you believe it, Yuval? Do your friends believe it?

YUVAL: Sometimes. Some of them. It's what we eat. But then there are moments when I am putting my feet into clean socks or drinking cold water on a hot day and something falls somewhere in the house, and breaks and it sounds almost beautiful and then I feel a sharp. I don't know. A burning. And I just don't know anymore.

UM HISHAM: Tell your mother, when you see her, that I have something that belongs to her.

YUVAL: Just give it to me. She won't meet with you. I'll see she gets it. There are regulations on what we can carry. How much does it weigh?

UM HISHAM: I don't know.

YUVAL: How big is it?

UM HISHAM: About three minutes.

YUVAL: That's not size that's time.

UM HISHAM: And yet it is more precious to a mother than anything in the world.

YUVAL: Then give me the minutes that belong to my mother.

UM HISHAM turns away.

Hey. If they belong to her, give them back. We stole your land, you stole our minutes. Now give them back.

SHLOMO enters flustered.

SHLOMO: The soldiers wouldn't let me past to measure the new ruin. How the hell is an architect to get work when they won't let me inspect the property? An IDF soldier has been killed there. They are investigating.

YUVAL: How did he die?

SHLOMO: A bullet from a Rafah sniper. In the head.

UM HISHAM: My daughter Asma was eleven years old. She was always counting.

YUVAL: Shit. A fellow soldier down. You see, you people are murderers.

UM HISHAM: My husband and I used to tease her that she was born with a book in her head, a book of numbers. But this did not make her a sour child. On the contrary, she was always laughing and at the end of the day she'd say 'Mother, you have taken one thousand forty-four steps in the kitchen today.' Or 'Father, you have pulled on your ear seventeen times this afternoon.' And 'Look at me, I have made eighty-three circles in the air with my toe!' She had six pigeons. She named them One, Two, Three, Four, Five –

YUVAL: and Six.

UM HISHAM: No. After Five came Nine. Nine was a surprise. Like Asma, always a suprise. An Israeli bullet. To the head. Except she was not carrying a gun and shooting children. She was on the roof, tending her pigeons.

YUVAL: You're right. I never wanted to be a soldier.

SHLOMO: I fought for a splendid cause, in another age, another land. I miss it.

UM HISHAM: This is our land. An Israeli soldier does not belong on our land.

SHLOMO: I cannot cry any longer. Too much dust in my eyes. See?

YUVAL: Get out of my zoo. Both of you. It's beginning to get dark. The screaming will start. Pieces of the animals will begin to fall off. You don't want to see it. Only a soldier's got the guts for this business. (*Beat.*) I'm sorry about your daughter.

UM HISHAM slaps YUVAL.

UM HISHAM: I don't want your sorry. I could not hold her. Bleeding among the feathers and bird shit. Was she afraid? Did she call out for me? As she lay on her back, dying, what did she count? The noises in the sky hanging over her? Or the beats of her draining heart? I know Asma so I know she counted something. I can't sleep for thinking about it. But what? What do you think she counted?

YUVAL: I don't know.

UM HISHAM: Make a wild guess, soldier.

YUVAL: Her breath.

UM HISHAM: Shut your mouth now.

YUVAL: Maybe she counted her breath. In and out. In and out.

UM HISHAM: In and out. Maybe. But I will never know. What I know is Asma died alone.

(*Says in Arabic.*) For this I will never forgive even God.

SHLOMO: Um Hisham. I too am sorry about your daughter. Death is not a part of my architectual plan. Though sometimes it happens, it just spills out...

UM HISHAM: Leave us, Shlomo.

SHLOMO: I would like to stay a little while.

UM HISHAM: Not now. Your ruins are missing you. Go.

SHLOMO: Yes, we see eye to eye, the ruins and I. (*Beat.*) Yet all I see are ruins. Ah well, Homa Umigdal, Homa –

UM HISHAM: Come and see me again tomorrow. You know I always expect you.

SHLOMO nods, then says some quiet words to her in Arabic: 'And I will always expect you, Um Hisham. Let us go with God.' Then he leaves.

YUVAL: He speaks Arabic?

UM HISHAM: Of course he does. When you get that old all languages possess you. Now I must go too. I'll be back tomorrow.

YUVAL: Give your family my condolences. I mean that. From my heart.

UM HISHAM: Yes. I believe you do. Give my condolences to your mother.

YUVAL steps back, startled.

YUVAL: Why?

UM HISHAM just looks at him some moments.

UM HISHAM: It's a terrible thing to lose a child.

YUVAL: My mother hasn't lost a child. How dare you?

UM HISHAM: Yuval.

YUVAL: Are you threatening my family? Are you fucking threatening my family?

UM HISHAM: I have thought of sending your mother a bouquet but I am too angry and I hate the smell of flowers. So just tell your mother I think of her. I don't want to, but I do. We had pieces of life, in common. In our children. Our children were our pieces of life. Now we have pieces of death. In common.

YUVAL: No.

UM HISHAM: I'm sorry.

YUVAL: No.

UM HISHAM: It's alright.

YUVAL: You're a liar!

UM HISHAM just looks at YUVAL.

I am alive, you hear me! I am alive. I am alive! (*Shouts.*) I am alive!

They both are silent some moments. As UM HISHAM speaks, just telling the story not reliving it, YUVAL listens quietly.

UM HISHAM: You came to my house in Rafah at five thirty a.m., with two other soldiers. You broke down the door. Your friends found no weapons in my house. How could they? We had none. Your friends were bored so they began to beat my husband. He was on the ground. They kicked him in the chest seven times. If Asma had been there she would have counted. But then you stopped them. Why did you stop them?

YUVAL just looks at her.

I was so grateful that I made you a cup of tea. And you accepted. You stood in the hallway, the dawn light from the broken door rushing past you. You put the cup to your lips. (*Beat.*) A single bullet from a sniper. To the head. You went down on one knee, still holding the cup. You looked at me as though it were a joke – all of it – that moment, the tea spilling across your thighs, the orange birds on the tiled floor, my face so close to your face. You said –

YUVAL: (*Quietly.*) Don't. I don't want to know what I said.

UM HISHAM: You said –

YUVAL: I don't want to know.

UM HISHAM: Hold me. And you kept saying it:

YUVAL: (*Quietly.*) Hold me. Hold me. Hold me.

UM HISHAM: Three minutes. It took you three minutes to die. Everything I have despised, for decades – the uniform, the power, the brutality, the inhumanity – and I held it in my arms. I held you, Yuval, and God forgive me I held you as I would have held my own child. (*Beat.*) But it should have been your mother. We should hold our own children when they die.

After some moments.

YUVAL: Then I am in hell.

UM HISHAM: No, Yuval. You are in the Rafah zoo. The one that still lives in our minds. And every day I'll come here and visit you, as I visit my daughter.

YUVAL: They bulldozed your house because I died there.

UM HISHAM: Yes.

YUVAL: They arrested your husband.

UM HISHAM: Yes.

YUVAL: Will you really come see me every day?

UM HISHAM: I have no choice.

YUVAL: Plato said 'He whom love touches not, walks in darkness.' Its not dark here. Not always. Does that mean I walk in love?

UM HISHAM: It's what I hope. For your sake.

YUVAL: Alright. (*Beat.*) Well, I need to go feed the porcupine. We've become pretty close, as close as a soldier and a porcupine can get. Wait. Before you go. That song you were singing earlier. I know it. How fucking ironic, huh, that I'd heard it before. You sang it as I died.

UM HISHAM: Yes.

YUVAL: Please. Sing it for me. Again.

UM HISHAM: No.

UM HISHAM shakes her head and she starts to leave. But then she sits down and begins to sing, the same song she sang at the opening. Her voice is strong and echoes across the zoo. YUVAL lays his rifle down elswhere on stage. He slowly goes down on one knee, then he lies down, face up, near UM HISHAM. After a few moments of listening to her sing, YUVAL slowly moves crawls closer to UM HISHAM and then carefully puts his head in her lap. Then YUVAL closes his eyes. She puts one arm lightly across his chest as she continues to sing.

End.